# CREATIVE THINKING IN BUSINESS

# CREATIVE THINKING IN BUSINESS

## A Practical Guide

**Carol Kinsey Goman**

KOGAN
PAGE

First published in the United States of America in 1989 by Crisp Publications Inc, 95 First Street, Los Altos, California 94022, USA.

This edition first published in Great Britain in 1989 by Kogan Page Ltd, 120 Pentonville Road, London N1 9JN

**British Library Cataloguing in Publication Data**

Goman, Carol Kinsey
    Creative thinking in business.
    1. Management. Creative thought
    I. Title
    658.4′03

ISBN 0-7494-0057-9
ISBN 0-7494-0058-7 Pbk

Typeset by the Castlefield Press, Wellingborough, Northants.
Printed and bound in Great Britain by
Biddles Limited, Guildford

# Contents

# To the Reader

According to a recent survey, when senior managers were asked to state the most important and valued traits in workers, they said *creative problem-solving and new ideas*. In business, creative thinking can help you to launch major projects or untangle minor snarl-ups. It provides fresh insight into and new perspectives on even the most routine elements of your job. Best of all, it enables you to regard problem-solving as a creative opportunity!

Sounds like magic? While it can work wonders for you, creativity isn't some mystical force or extraordinary talent possessed by the lucky few. Rather, it is an ability everyone (to some degree or another) has. Even better, it is also a skill you can develop more fully.

This book was designed to help you uncover more of your innate creative potential, and go on to develop techniques that will allow you to 'tune in' to your creativity at will.

Each chapter of *Creative Thinking in Business* leads to a better understanding how how you can become a better generator of ideas and innovative problem-solver. The chapters are:

1. Getting Started
2. Creativity Blocks and Blockbusters
3. Techniques for Idea Generation
4. Group Creativity
5. Innovation and Practical Solutions

Learning to use more of your creativity will allow you to

rekindle that spark of excitement about work, to have more confidence in your ability to confront situations with fresh ideas and innovative solutions, and to take advantage of the creative input of others.

Carol Kinsey Goman

# About This Book

*Creative Thinking in Business* is unlike most books. It's not a book to read – it's a book to use. The unique 'self-paced' format of this book and its worksheets encourage the reader to get involved and try some new ideas immediately.

The object of this book is to help those in business to develop and use more creative ability in their daily work. Using the simple yet sound techniques presented can make a dramatic difference to one's personal and professional success.

This book (and the other Better Management Skills titles included in the list on page 89) can be used effectively in a number of ways. Here are some possibilities:

*Individual study.* Because the book is self-instructional, all that is needed is a quiet place, some time and a pencil. Completing the activities and exercises will provide valuable feedback, as well as practical ideas you can use immediately on the job.

*Workshops and seminars.* The book is ideal as assigned reading before a workshop or seminar. With the basics in hand, the quality of participation will improve, and more time can be spent on extending and applying the concept during the programme. The book is also effective when it is handed out at the beginning of a session, and participants 'work through' the contents.

*Open learning.* Books can be used by those not able to attend head office training sessions.

# CHAPTER 1
# Getting Started

## What is true creativity?

Years ago in the US newspaper comic strip, *'Ripley's Believe It or Not'*, the following item appeared: A plain iron bar is worth $5.00. If you take that iron bar and forge horseshoes from it, the value increases to $10.50. If it's made into needles, the price rises to $3,285.00. And if you make watch springs from it, it then is worth £250,000.00. Ergo, the difference between $5.00 and $250,000.00 is creativity.

Sounds like sense? Take a closer look. A horseshoe made of iron would wear out in a week. Horseshoes are made of steel and so are needles – and you cannot make an iron bar into watch springs.

Things are not always what they seem. Logical thought and sound common sense should always form the basis from which true creativity springs.

## Definitions

- **Creativity.** Bringing into existence an idea that is new to you.
- **Innovation.** The practical application of creative ideas.
- **Creative thinking.** An innate talent that you were born with *and* a set of skills that can be learned, developed and used in daily problem-solving.
- **Creative people.** Those people who do not suppress their innate creativity and who use their creative ability in various aspects of life.

All of us can enhance the creativity we possess.

## You are creative already

In what areas of life do you display your creativity? (Hobby, work, relationships, public speaking, art, music, crafts, etc)

_____

_____

_____

_____

Where have your creative ideas been put to practical use? (Party you gave, report or project you designed, unique approach to a presentation, etc)

_____

_____

_____

_____

What was the most creative thing you did as a child?

_____

_____

_____

_____

In what area of your life would you like to be more creative?

_____

_____

_____

_____

What people (living or dead) are or were creative in ways that impressed you?

_____

_____

_____

_____

## Your IQ (Intelligence Quotient) is not your CQ (Creativity Quotient)

The late Dr Richard Feynman was one of the world's leading theoretical physicists. After being awarded the Nobel Prize in Sweden, he flew to his home town and stopped at his old school. While he was there he looked up his class marks. They were not as good as he had remembered, so he asked to see his IQ score. It was 124 – only slightly above average. He was delighted. 'Winning a Nobel Prize is no big deal,' he reportedly told his wife, 'but winning it with an IQ of 124 is really something!'

## How high is your Creativity Quotient?

Complete the following questionnaire to check your Creativity Quotient. Score 3 for always, 2 for sometimes, 1 for once in a while, 0 for never.

_____ 1. Are you curious? Are you interested in other people's opinions, problems from other departments, customer feedback?

_____ 2. Are you a 'creative opportunist?' Do you find opportunities for solving problems, creating wants, filling needs?

_____ 3. Are you a strategist? Do you spend time redefining your goals, revising plans to reach them or using organisational changes creatively in order to benefit your own career?

_____ 4. Are you a challenger? Do you examine assumptions biases, or preconceived beliefs for loopholes and opportunities?

_____ 5. Are you a trend spotter? Do you actively monitor change in your field, such as technology government regulations, or new management strategies to spot opportunities early?

_____ 6. Are you a connector or an adaptor? Do you keep your eyes open for concepts you can borrow from one field and apply to another?

_____ 7. Are you a risk taker? Are you willing to develop and experiment with ideas of your own?

_____ 8. How is your intuition? Do you rely on your guesses and insights?

_____ 9. Are you a simplifier? Can you reduce complex decisions to a few simple questions by seeing the overall view?

_____ 10. Are you an 'idea seller'? Can you promote and gather support for your ideas?

_____ 11. Are you a visionary? Do you think further ahead than most of your colleagues? Do you think long term? Do you share your vision with others?

_____ 12. Are you resourceful? Do you dig out research and information to support your ideas?

_____ 13. Are you supportive of the creative ideas from your peers and subordinates? Do you welcome 'better ideas' from others?

_____ 14. Does your creativity extend to others? Do you have colleagues with whom you share creative ideas for feedback and support?

_____ 15. Are you a futurist? Do you attend lectures or read books about the 'cutting edge' in your field? Are you fascinated by the future?

_____ 16. Do you believe that you are a creative thinker? Do you have faith in your own good ideas?

_____ Score

This questionnaire was adapted from _How to Motivate People_ by Twyla Dell (Kogan Page).

A score of 41–48 shows you have a very high creativity quotient. You will find creative ways to put the techniques in this book to use! 36–40 shows you're mentally ready to explore more of your creativity, and should do very well using the techniques and exercises presented. 30–35 indicates that you have yet to discover your true creative capacity. By practising some of the ideas in the book you should be greatly encouraged by the positive results. Below 29 you may be surprised by the increase in your creativity after using this book. You don't know yet how creative you can be!

# CHAPTER 2
# Creativity Blocks and Blockbusters

## You were born to be creative

In the late 1940s, a group of psychologists were discussing the lack of creativity in most adults. They speculated that by the age of 45, only a minute percentage of the population could think creatively. To prove that assumption they designed a creativity test and gave it to a group of 45-year-olds. Less than 5 per cent of them were judged creative by the test.

They continued testing by reducing the age of the subjects. They tested at ages 40, 35, 30, 25 and 20 years old. The 5 per cent creativity figure stayed basically the same for all these groups. Finally, at 17 years old the percentage of creative individuals rose to 10 per cent. At the age of five, it rocketed to over 90 per cent! The conclusion? Almost everyone is highly creative at the age of five.

## Benefits from enhancing your creativity

Tick the boxes opposite those statements that you believe to be true for you.

Increasing your creativity at work can:

☐ Help you to make the best use of your talents, aptitudes and abilities.

☐ Enhance the enjoyment of your job.

☐ Improve your self-confidence.

☐ Make you a more valuable employee.

☐ Enhance your opinion of yourself as a proficient problem-solver.

☐ Ultimately increase your income.

☐ Make you more self-motivated.

☐ Help you to feel more innovative and 'entrepreneurial'.

☐ Give you a greater sense of control and mastery over your job.

If you ticked even one box, it should motivate you to learn the techniques demonstrated in this book to increase your CQ.

## Blocks and blockbusters to creativity

### Blocks to creativity

- Negative attitude
- Fear of failure
- Executive stress
- Following rules
- Assumptions
- Over-reliance on logic
- Believing you are not creative

### Creativity blockbusters

- Attitude adjustment
- Risk-taking techniques
- Stress safety valves
- Breaking the rules
- Checking assumptions
- Your 'internal' creative climate
- Creative beliefs

Discover what blocks your creativity – then develop a block-busting strategy!

*Block 1*
## Negative attitude

In Chinese, the ideogram for 'crisis' combines two characters: one is the symbol for danger, the other for opportunity. The pessimist by nature will turn his or her attention to the negative aspects of a problem and expend creative energy worrying about possible unsatisfactory outcomes. The optimist, on the other hand, will display creativity by concentrating on the inherent opportunities. What is your attitude?

*Blockbuster 1*
## Attitude adjustment scale

Rate your current attitude. Read each statement and circle the number where you feel you belong. If you circle a 10, this indicates that your attitude could not be better in this area; if you circle a 1, it could not be worse. Be honest with yourself.

|  | **HIGH** (Positive) | **LOW** (Negative) |
|---|---|---|
| 1. If I had to guess, I think my boss would currently rate my attitude as | 10 9 8 7 6 5 4 3 2 1 | |
| 2. Given the same chance, my colleagues and family would rate my current attitude as | 10 9 8 7 6 5 4 3 2 1 | |
| 3. Realistically, I would rate my current attitude as | 10 9 8 7 6 5 4 3 2 1 | |
| 4. If there were a meter that could gauge my sense of humour, I'd rate | 10 9 8 7 6 5 4 3 2 1 | |
| 5. My recent disposition – the patience and consideration I show to others – deserves a rating of | 10 9 8 7 6 5 4 3 2 1 | |
| 6. My attitude towards my own ideas and creativity is | 10 9 8 7 6 5 4 3 2 1 | |
| 7. My attitude towards other people's creative ideas is | 10 9 8 7 6 5 4 3 2 1 | |

|  | HIGH<br>(Positive) | LOW<br>(Negative) |
|---|---|---|
| 8. Lately, my ability to generate lots of possible solutions has been | 10 9 8 7 6 5 4 3 2 1 | |
| 9. I would rate my enthusiasm towards my job during the past few weeks as | 10 9 8 7 6 5 4 3 2 1 | |
| 10. I would rate my enthusiasm about my life in general to be | 10 9 8 7 6 5 4 3 2 1 | |

TOTAL _____

---

A score of 90 or over is a signal that your attitude is 'in tune' and no adjustments seem necessary; a score between 70 and 90 indicates that minor adjustments may help; a rating between 50 and 70 suggests a major adjustment; if you rated below 50, a complete overhaul may be required.

---

This scale was adapted from *How to Develop a Positive Attitude* by Elwood N Chapman (Kogan Page).

## Block 2
## Fear of failure

Fear of failure is one of the greatest inhibitors of natural creativity, and yet every successful innovator has failed often. Tom Watson, the founder of IBM, was often quoted as saying, 'The way to accelerate your success is to double your failure rate.' Tom Peters, the management guru, declares that the prescription for dramatically speeded-up innovation is dramatically increased rates of failure. Those who embrace failure as a by-product of creativity definitely have the advantage!

## Blockbuster 2
## Risk-taking technique

1. What creative risk are you currently considering?

2. Why is it important for you to take this risk?

3. If you took this risk and failed, what would be the worst possible outcome?

4. If this approach failed, what are your other options?

5. How do you plan to deal with this failure?

*Case Study 1*
# Fear of failure

A woman in her thirties, Vicky was being groomed by her father to take over the family business. Vicky told her best friend: 'This is such a wonderful opportunity. I have so many new ideas about how to improve the business. I only hope that I don't let him down!'

The friend replied: 'What would happen if you tried your best and still failed to live up to your father's expectations? What if he didn't like your ideas?'

Startled, she replied, 'Why, I'd feel perfectly awful!' Then her friend asked: 'What would you do after you felt awful?'

Vicky ran through an entire sequence of reactions. She fantasised about leaving the district, changing her name, and finally joked about putting herself 'up for adoption'. At last she smiled and said, 'I'd just have to find a way to survive.'

Based on her response, do you think Vicky is a creative person?

☐ ☐
Yes  No

*Block 3*
**Excessive stress**

Psychologically, an over-stressed person finds it increasingly difficult to be objective and has trouble seeing alternatives. This is often accompanied by a tremendous sense of being under pressure based on feelings such as not enough time, too many demands, or being trapped. Distressful emotions such as these will usually result in poor creative thinking and reduced decision-making abilities.

*Blockbuster 3*
**Safety valves for stress**

Tick the appropriate column. Rate yourself honestly.

| Doing very well | Average | Need improvement | |
|---|---|---|---|
| 5 | 3 | 1 | I am succeeding at: |
| _____ | _____ | _____ | 1. Taking responsibility for my own stress. (not blaming others) |
| _____ | _____ | _____ | 2. Knowing my optimum level of stress. (where you do your best) |
| _____ | _____ | _____ | 3. Balancing work and play. |
| _____ | _____ | _____ | 4. Relaxing more. (learning when it's appropriate to do nothing) |
| _____ | _____ | _____ | 5. Getting enough sleep. |
| _____ | _____ | _____ | 6. Refusing to take on more than I can handle. |
| _____ | _____ | _____ | 7. Exercising regularly. |
| _____ | _____ | _____ | 8. Setting realistic goals. |
| _____ | _____ | _____ | 9. Practising relaxation exercises. |
| _____ | _____ | _____ | 10. Taking pleasure in the here and now. |
| _____ | _____ | _____ | 11. Valuing family and friends. |
| _____ | _____ | _____ | 12. Managing my time and setting priorities. |
| _____ | _____ | _____ | 13. Finding time for recreation and hobbies. |
| _____ | _____ | _____ | 14. Avoiding too much caffeine. |
| _____ | _____ | _____ | 15. Making sure I have a proper diet. |
| _____ | _____ | _____ | 16. Avoiding alcohol or other substances as a means of dealing with pressure. |
| _____ | _____ | _____ | 17. Avoiding emotional 'overload'. (taking on other people's problems when under stress) |

| Doing very well | Average | Need improvement |
|:---:|:---:|:---:|
| 5 | 3 | 1 |

_____ _____ _____ 18. Giving and accepting positive signs of appreciation.

_____ _____ _____ 19. Talking through troubles and getting professional help if needed.

_____ _____ _____ 20. Taking more care before making emotional 'investments'.

_____ _____ _____ 21. Taking breaks at work when needed.

Score _____

---

If your score was between 21 and 50, there are several areas you need to develop better to release your stress. It might be a good idea to discuss some of your answers with a counsellor or close friend.

If you scored between 51 and 75, you have discovered a variety of ways to deal effectively with stress. Make a note of those items for which you ticked 'Need improvement' and work out ways which will help you move to the 'Average' box.

If your score was 75 or more – congratulations. You have found some excellent ways of dealing with the frustrations and complexities of life.

---

_Block 4_
## Following the rules

While some rules are obviously necessary (ie we should all be happy that there is consensus about stopping at red lights), others hinder innovation because they encourage a mentally lazy acceptance of the status quo. Many inventions and innovations in a particular industry have come from people outside that industry. Why? Because the people who make the creative breakthroughs are not hampered by knowing all the rules and limitations.

*Blockbuster 4*
## Breaking the rules

It is not always a bad idea to break certain rules – especially the ones which govern your daily routine. Which of the following 'rule breakers' would you like to try? (Mark it with an X and write the date you intend to put it into practice.)

| Rule breaker | Date |
|---|---|
| _____ Take a different route to work. | _____ |
| _____ Have lunch at new restaurant. | _____ |
| _____ Try a different kind of food for lunch. | _____ |
| _____ Skip lunch and go swimming or jogging. | _____ |
| _____ Ask for something outlandish. | _____ |
| _____ Come to work in the morning and pretend it is your first day there. Note down your reactions. | _____ |
| _____ Come to work in the morning and pretend you are a customer or a competitor. Then write down your reations. | _____ |
| _____ Enrol for an activity you have never tried before. | _____ |
| _____ Invite someone you don't know to have lunch or a conversation with you. | _____ |
| _____ Read a book on a topic about which you know nothing. | _____ |
| _____ Go somewhere you have never been before for the weekend. | _____ |
| _____ Ask for advice or information from someone whose opinion you have never sought (spouse, child, caretaker, client, stranger). | _____ |
| _____ Stand facing the rear of the lift. | _____ |

What other rules would you like to break?          **Date**

_____     _____

_____     _____

_____     _____

_____     _____

_____     _____

_____     _____


What prevents you from breaking them?

_____

_____

_____

_____

_____

_____

_____


*Block 5*
**Making assumptions**

A recent story told how the research and development manager of a large high-tech firm found supplies and test equipment missing from a laboratory store, so he ordered a security system to be installed. Several months passed without any further losses.

While preparing a routine report for the company chairman, the manager noticed that progress on a couple of key projects had slowed down. Concerned, he decided to investigate. He discovered that several technical research engineers had stopped working on the projects at home at weekends because they could no longer get supplies and test equipment. The R & D manager had mistakenly assumed the missing supplies were taken by dishonest employees. He had therefore 'solved' the wrong problem. Making iron-clad assumptions often inhibits creative thinking about other possibilities.

*Blockbuster 5*
## Checking assumptions

To avoid solving the wrong problem while at the same time opening your creative thinking to possible solutions, it is wise to check your assumptions. Begin by asking yourself questions like:

- What are the most likely possibilities?
- What am I taking for granted?
- What are some other possible explanations?

For example, you are at a library and you see a woman put two books in her bag and begin to walk out. What are the possible assumptions?

1. She is stealing the books.
2. She is the librarian.
3. They are her books.

What else?

4. _____
5. _____
6. _____

What could you do to find out if one of the possible assumptions is accurate? (Write your response in the space provided below.)

Based on each assumption from the exercise on the previous page, what would a possible solution be? (Notice that each assumption leads to a different variety of solutions.)

Can you think of any situation at work where your assumptions might be leading you to solve the wrong problem?

How can you check for accuracy?

It always makes sense to check your assumptions.


**Nine dot puzzle**

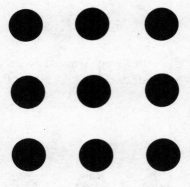

The instructions are to draw four straight lines that go through all nine dots by never taking your pen or pencil off the paper. If you have trouble doing this, check your *assumptions* about the *rules*. Can you find the solution? If you are really creative, the nine dot puzzle can be solved with three straight lines.

(The solution is given overleaf.)

## Solutions

To solve the puzzle with four straight lines, you must challenge your assumption that the 'rules' meant you had to stay within the dots.

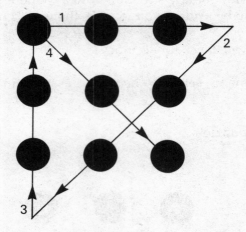

To solve the puzzle with three straight lines, you don't have to go through the centre of each dot! (At least the rules do not so specify.)

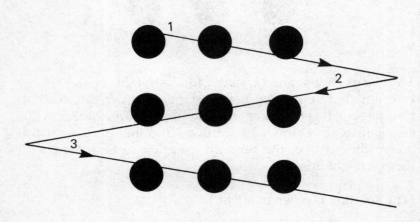

*Block 6*
## Over-reliance on logic

Dr Jonas Salk, developer of the Salk vaccine, said, 'When I became a scientist, I would picture myself as a virus or cancer cell and try to image what it would be like to be either.' Einstein wrote that 'Imagination is more powerful than knowledge.'

Highly creative thinkers see the advantage of going beyond logical problem-solving techniques to include imagination, intuition, emotion and/or humour.

*Blockbuster 6*
## Your 'internal' creative climate
1. Write out one problem you have been trying to solve using a purely logical approach.

2. Stay open-minded and with a positive mental attitude, close your eyes and let your body relax. State the problem clearly to yourself.

3. Turn the situation over to your imagination, your intuition, your feelings and your sense of humour. Play with possibilities, insights, absurdities. Don't judge your thoughts, just let them come.

4. Write out key words or thoughts until you feel yourself reaching out for additional ideas.

5. Flesh our your ideas by writing for five or ten minutes – allow one thought to lead to another.

6. Retrace your steps to 'play with' and discover additional aspects.

*Block 7*
## Believing you are not creative

Ninety per cent of knowledge about the human brain and creativity has been discovered in the past ten years. Brain research indicates that the creative capacity of the human brain is potentially limitless. The only restrictions are the ones we impose ourselves through our system of beliefs.

The biggest obstacle you may ever have to face is an absolute acceptance of what you believe you can or cannot accomplish.

If you believe you can or if you believe you can't . . . you're right.

*Blockbuster 7*
**Creative beliefs**

The human brain is often compared to a computer; using this comparison, it is easy to see that creative results require creative programming!

List those beliefs about yourself that would help you to grow into a more creative person.

1.


2.


3.


4.


5.


6.


7.


8.


9.


10.

Some beliefs stand in the way of your creativity and you should make an attempt to rid yourself of them. List examples of your non-productive goals here.

1.

2.

3.

4.

5.

6.

7.

8.

9.

10.

When you have completed this list, take a marker and cross off each idea on the list. Whenever one of the limiting beliefs you wrote down comes into your thoughts, remember that you chose to eliminate it. Replace it with a more productive belief that you have decided to retain.

# 15 Ways to become more creative

Tick those you intend to use within the next month.
I plan to:

☐ 1. Ask 'what if' questions – the more ridiculous the better. (What if we all wore jeans to work? What if we got paid every day? What if my boss had to work for me one day a week?)

☐ 2. Make up metaphors and analogies. (A brain is like a bank – you can only take out as much as you put in. My job is like _____.

☐ 3. Pay attention to small ideas. That's how many big ones begin.

☐ 4. Daydream. Let your mind wander.

☐ 5. Play 'Just suppose.' (Just suppose I decided to ask for a rise . . .Just suppose I found a better way to serve our customers . . . Just suppose.)

☐ 6. Try out different ways of expressing your creativity (cooking, painting, photography, writing, playing tennis, inventing, giving parties, etc).

☐ 7. Notice when you do something creative and keep a CREATIVITY SUCCESS file.

☐ 8. Learn and play strategy games such as chess, draughts, backgammon or bridge.

☐ 9. Learn a foreign language (and force your brain to think in new patterns).

☐ 10. If you're right-handed, try using your left hand to do things. If you're left-handed, switch to your right for a while.

☐ 11. Guess at measurements rather than using a ruler, tape measure or jug. Then measure and see how close you were.

☐ 12. Balance your cheque book without using a calculator.

☐ 13. Read three-quarters of a novel, then stop and write your own ending.

☐ 14. Stand on your head to get the blood really flowing to your brain.

☐ 15. Do jigsaws and crossword puzzles.

# CHAPTER 3
# Techniques for Idea Generation

## What did you learn at school?

If you were to go into an average classroom of senior school students and draw a large dot on the biackboard, how do you think they'd answer the question, 'What is that?'

*Would you agree that the most likely answer would be, 'A dot!'*

Now what if you did the same thing in front of a kindergarten class? What answers do you suppose you'd hear?

Somewhere between the beginning and the end of our formal education, we have developed ways to find the 'right' answer, but lost the creative impetus to go beyond the other possible right answers.

## What helps or hinders?

Linus Pauling, the Nobel prizewinning scientist, said: 'The best way to get good ideas is to have lots of ideas.' Highly creative thinkers agree that the first step to becoming more innovative is to generate lots of possibilities.

Some habits and behaviour patterns encourage the production of ideas while others inhibit idea generation completely. Which of these actions are you most likely to do?

| **Hinders** | **Helps** |
|---|---|
| Do you usually: | or: |
| ____ look for the *right* answer | ____ look for lots of possible right answers |
| ____ approach problem-solving as a 'serious' business | ____ have fun with problem-solving and 'play' with ideas |
| ____ avoid making mistakes as far as possible | ____ accept mistakes as a natural by-product of the creative process |
| ____ push yourself even when tired to keep working on a problem | ____ take deliberate breaks when you put the problem on the back burner |
| ____ ask advice only from 'experts' | ____ get information from a variety of sources |
| ____ dismiss your 'silly' ideas | ____ use your sense of humour as a rich source of possibilities |

| Hinders | Helps |
|---|---|
| Do you usually: | or: |

| Hinders | Helps |
|---|---|
| ____ tell your ideas only to people who will agree with or support them | ____ encourage feedback from a variety of sources including a 'Devil's advocate' |
| ____ keep quiet when you don't understand something | ____ risk asking 'stupid' questions |
| ____ follow the motto 'If it isn't broken, it doesn't need mending' | ____ continually look for ways to improve all products, services and systems |
| ____ do not have a system of recording ideas that come to you | ____ keep an 'ideas notebook' to record all good ideas |

## The one-minute idea generator

In one minute, take a piece of paper and list as many uses for a paperclip as you can think of. Here are some suggestions to bear in mind:

1. Go for quantity, not quality of ideas.
2. Write down *every* idea. Do not judge or criticise!
3. Stay relaxed, playful, even silly.
4. Adapt your point of view. (Look at the paperclip as if you were an insect, as if you were lost in the desert, as if you were a designer, etc.)
5. Ask yourself 'What if?' questions. (What if the paperclip were straightened out and a hole drilled through the middle? What if a bunch of them were linked together? What if one end was sharpened to a point?)

Ready now, time yourself for one minute. *Ready — steady — go.*

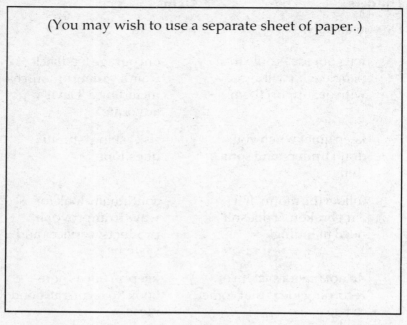

(You may wish to use a separate sheet of paper.)

How did you do? Were you able to keep writing for the whole minute? Did you run out of ideas? Or do you still have ideas coming?

## Idea-generating questions

An excellent technique for generating ideas is to use idea-generating questions. These can serve as a checklist for possibilities. When you use a checklist such as this, start with a particular item and think about ways to expand it.

1. What else could it be used for (without any changes)?
2. What could it be used for instead? What else is like this?
3. How could it be adapted or modified for a new use?
4. What if it were larger (thicker, heavier, stronger)?
5. What if it were smaller (thinner, lighter, shorter)?
6. How might it be rearranged (reversed)?
7. Etc.

*Example*

Imagine that the object you're thinking of is an umbrella. Using the checklist, complete the following exercise:

1. *What else could it be used for?*
   Possible answer – to dig holes.

   What else _____

   _____

   _____

2. *What could be used instead? What else is like this?*
   Possible answer – a newspaper held over your head.

   What else _____

   _____

   _____

3. *How could it be adapted for a new use?*
   Possible answer – add a torch to the handle for people who go out on a dark, rainy day.

   What else _____

   _____

   _____

4. *What if it were larger (thicker, heavier, stronger)?*
   Possible answer – make it twice the size to cover two people.

   What else _____

   _____

   _____

5. *What if it were smaller (thinner, lighter, shorter)?*
Possible answer – make it small enough to fold up and fit inside a handbag.

What else? _____

_____

_____

6. *How might it be rearranged (reversed)?*
Possible answer – turn it upside down and use it as a birdbath.

What else? _____

_____

_____

## Different points of view

Creative thinking begins with the generation of ideas. If you are to have the broadest perspective on a situation, at some point you will need to consider the different viewpoints of all the people involved. The skill of deliberately shifting your point of view to accommodate those of others will allow you to create a more complete list of the factors, consequences and options involved.

For example, if a chemical company is developing a new pesticide to increase crop yields, it would be to their advantage to consider the following points of view:

- *The farmer.* Interested in cost of product and how it is applied. Encouraged by reports of increased yield. Concerned about possible toxicity to people and animals.

- *The company.* Wants more information on production costs, the source of the ingredients, the potential market size, and the expected profit margin.

- *The consumer.* Worried about the effects of the product on health, taste of food and price to be paid in the market.

- *The environmentalist.* Concerned about pollution, contamination and the ecological effects on the food chain.

- *Others.* (Add your own.)

_____

_____

_____

_____

_____

_____

## Office automation exercise

Assume that you are the manager of a large personnel department and you want to automate by introducing computers for your entire office staff. Most have never used computers before. The office manager responsible for managing them has been with the company for 20 years. What do you suppose would be the different points of view when you announce your plan?

- Your boss:


- Your office manager:


- The office staff:


- Other departments in the organisation:


- Are there other points of view you should consider?

## Split brain theory

In 1981 Roger Sperry was awarded the Nobel Prize for his work on the split brain theory. According to Dr Sperry, the brain has two hemispheres with different but overlapping functions. The right and left hemispheres of the brain each specialise in distinct types of thinking processes.

In general, in 95 per cent of all right-handed people, the left side of the brain not only cross-controls the right side of the body, but is also responsible for analytical, linear, verbal and rational thought. (In most left-handed people, the hemispheric functions are reversed.) It is a left-brain function you rely on when balancing your cheque book, remembering names and dates, or setting goals and objectives. Since most of our concepts of thinking come from Greek logic, left-brained processes are most rewarded in our education system.

The right hemisphere controls the left side of the body and is holistic, imaginative, non-verbal, and artistic. Whenever you think of someone's face, become engrossed in a symphony, or simply daydream, you are engaging in right-brain function. Right-brain processes are less often rewarded at school.

# Left hemisphere                    Right hemisphere

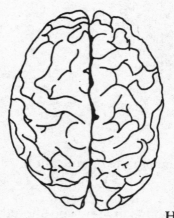

Logic

Sequential

Verbal

Linear

Analytical

Rational

Explicit

Intuition

Non-verbal

Visual

Spacial

Creative

Holistic

Artistic

Humorous/Playful

# Whole brain problem-solving

Creative problem-solvers understand that both hemispheres of the brain (both thinking processes) are valuable. The trick lies in knowing which function best supports a particular phase of the problem-solving process.

**Left.** Logically defines the problem

**Right.** Generates creative possibilities and alternative solutions.

**Left.** Pragmatically evaluates to determine which are applicable.

**Left.** Prepares a strategic plan for gaining support and imple-menting the solution.

**Right.** Persuades others by sharing your ideas and enthusiasm.

In the phase of generating ideas, right-brain functions are most helpful. Have you ever struggled to solve a problem and found the answer 'popped' into your head while you were out shopping or jogging or when you woke up the next day. That is because it was released from left-brain control and turned over to your right-brain insight.

The manager of human resources at a certain manufacturing company generates ideas most effectively when she is meditating. The director of strategic planning at a large communications company gets his best ideas when out running. A marketing representative likes to 'sleep on it', telling himself he'll have fresh ideas in the morning. A sales-person tells jokes and laughs her way into new insights. None of these people are aware they are shifting brain hemisphere function. All of them simply know (from trial and error) how to get the results they need.

Where do you get your best ideas?

_____

_____

_____

_____

_____

_____

## The creative ideas journal

To capture good ideas whenever and wherever they occur, take a pocket-sized notebook and write this question at the top of page 1: 'In what ways can I . . . ? (fill in your own problem). Put the notebook in your handbag or pocket. Without thinking about it, let your unconscious mind get to work on the problem and deliver possible solutions as they come into your mind throughout the day. Write down each idea with the time of day it occurred and the activity you were engaged in at that moment. By the end of the week, you will not only have several usable ideas, you will also know more about your creative 'schedule'.

---

### IDEAS JOURNAL
#### 'IN WHAT WAYS CAN I . . .

---

## Intuition

- The chairman of a large restaurant chain astounded his staff when he decided to build a restaurant in a run-down warehouse area. Two years later the new restaurant was the chain's top money-maker and the neighbourhood around it was revitalised.

- The chairman of a small Australian airline company telephones his treasurer frequently and tells him to get ready to buy replacement equipment. With days, one of the airline's planes unexpectedly needs a costly part.

- A plant manager of a leading US software company spends most of her time sitting at her desk doing paperwork. But every so often she gets up from her desk, and for reasons not clear to her, goes over to a point on the production line and picks out a software diskette and looks all right but turns out to be flawed.

Whether from a hunch, gut feeling, or even ESP, thousands of managers and executives make business deals based on intuition. Think back over your life. Have you ever had a hunch that you should or should not be doing something? If we are normal, we all have hunches, but many of us ignore or distrust them as being irrational and useless.

Creative thinkers tend to pay more attention to their feelings, including what they call their 'inner voice'. Management professor Weston Agor studied hundreds of top managers and found a disproportionate percentage used intuition as an important part of their decision-making process. Most managers first digested all the relevant information and data available, but when the data was conflicting or incomplete, they relied on intuitive approaches in order to reach a conclusion.

# How intuitive are you?

Answer the next ten questions by indicating whether you agree or disagree with each statement.

| | Yes | No |
|---|---|---|
| 1. I believe in ESP (extra-sensory perception). | __ | __ |
| 2. I have, on occasions, known exactly what was going to happen beforehand. | __ | __ |
| 3. I trust my instincts when I meet someone for the first time | __ | __ |
| 4. I often have flashes of insight about an important project | __ | __ |
| 5. Many of my best decisions were made by 'going along with a gut feeling'. | __ | __ |
| 6. I can often sense a problem before anyone tells me there is one. | __ | __ |
| 7. I have days when I do well just because I feel especially lucky. | __ | __ |
| 8. I have had what others would call a psychic experience. | __ | __ |
| 9. Sometimes the answer to a problem comes to me in a dream. | __ | __ |
| 10. If all the data supported one opinion and my intuition led me strongly to a conflicting decision, I would follow my intuition. | __ | __ |

---

*Yes* scores of 5 or more indicate a high reliance on intuition.
*No* scores of 5 or more show a low reliance on intuition.

---

## Ways to increase your business intuition

1. **Practise foretelling the future.** If you are going to a business meeting with people you haven't met before, guess how they'll look, what they'll be wearing and how they will approach the business in hand. If you're looking for a parking space, anticipate where the first vacant space will be.

2. **Imagine yourself doing a task before it comes up.** Not only will you prime your brain for actually doing the task, you will be able to compare your actual performance with the image in your mind.

3. **Notice feelings and inner sensations you usually ignore.** Pay attention to internal stirring and feelings. By monitoring them constantly, you are more likely to notice those changes that indicate something has registered unconsciously.

4. **Keep an ideas journal.** Write down any flashes of insight you have and keep a record of decisions you made on the basis of them. When you look at this 'diary' later on, you'll be able to assess how accurate you were.

5. **Meditate or learn self-hypnosis.** Insights are most likely to occur when you first make an effort is empty your conscious mind, then concentrate (fix your attention on one thing) and you will be more receptive to creative ideas bubbling up through the subconscious.

6. **Visualise symbolically.** When faced with a problem person or situation, create a mental picture that is symbolically representative. (For example, a nurse visualised her confrontations with the hospital's administration as Don Quixote tilting at windmills.) Notice any new creative ideas that come to you as a result of looking at your situation in a unique way.

# Creative imagination

This exercise requires at least two people; one to guide the process and one or more to participate.

**Step 1.** The participant(s) begin by choosing a specific problem or issue for which they would like additional insights and possibilities.

**Step 2.** The guide reads the following script slowly:

**Script**

**Guide.** 'Find a comfortable position, either sitting or lying down. Close your eyes and turn your attention to your breathing. Breathe in deeply (*Pause*) Now breathe out. (*Repeat several times*) Every time you breathe out, think the word RELAX. Let yourself start to release any physical tension you feel and imagine a flow of relaxation throughout your body, from the top of your head to the tips of your toes. (*Pause for a few seconds*) Let yourself relax deeply . . . comfortably . . . completely. Now as I count from 10 to 1, imagine yourself going down in a lift . . . a very special lift . . . going further down with every number I count. (*Count slowly*) 10 - 9 - 8 - 7 - 6 - 5 - 4 - 3 - 2 - 1. As you get out, you enter a very special room. It is your CREATIVITY ROOM, decorated just the way you like it . . . with furniture, colours, wall decorations and equipment of your choice. You feel instantly safe and at home here.' (*Pause for a few seconds*)

In a moment you will hear a knock on the door announcing the arrival of your CREATIVITY CONSULTANT. This may be someone you know and have consciously chosen to assist you. Or your counsellor may have been chosen subconsciously, and you will be surprised when that person appears. In any event, your counsellor is symbolic of your creative potential. (*Pause*) Now you hear the knock and go to the door to greet your consultant. (*Pause*) Open the door. (*Pause*)

Invite your consultant into the room and explain your problem situation in detail. (*Pause*) Ask your consultant for any advice or insight. (*Pause*) Pay attention if your consultant speaks to you. Be receptive to any idea or feeling that occurs. Notice whatever happens. (*Pause*) Ask your consultant for a single word that can help you to solve your problem. Listen carefully. (*Pause*) If you hear nothing, just clear your mind and let the first word you think of become your clue. Don't be concerned if there is no obvious connection between this word and your problem. Just accept whatever comes to you as having some hidden value. (*Pause*)

Now thank your consultant and say goodbye. Look around your room one last time. (*Pause*) Think about the word clue that was given to you as you leave your room and enter the lift. As I count from 1 to 10, feel yourself coming back to the present time and place. (*Count slowly*) 1 - 2 - 3 - 4 - 5 - 6 - 7 - 8 - 9 - 10. Open your eyes and say your clue word.

**Step 3.** Write your word on a blank sheet of paper. Immediately write whatever thoughts come to you. Relate this word to your problem situation. Use free association and write nonstop for at least five minutes.

## Phases of creativity

**1. Preparation.** Laying the groundwork. Gathering research, background information, specific data, various opinions.

**2. Concentration.** Becoming totally absorbed in the problem or situation.

**3. Incubation.** Taking time off, enjoying a rest period where the total process is turned over to the subconscious mind. Seeking distractions.

**4. Illumination.** The AHA! experience where insights, possibilities and answers come. Getting that great idea!

**5. Evaluation.** Testing your ideas by taking them through a checklist of criteria for practical application. Getting feedback, checking, assumptions through a pilot project, modifying and improving, gathering support.

**6. Application.** Innovatively applying the solution. Confronting and solving the problem by using your creativity.

## Metaphorical thinking

Many creative thinkers naturally gravitate towards the use of metaphors and analogies in their everyday speech and thought patterns. As a result, their perceptions of situations are normally more colourful and original.

Metaphor has long been accepted as a potent tool for the creative worker. Aristotle wrote that 'the greatest thing by far is to be the master of metaphor'. He regarded metaphoric ability (which implies the discernment of linkages between dissimilar objects and conditions) as a mark of genius.

Rules, regulations, and conventions give us order and security. With them we tend to shy away from that which is unknown, strange or different. One way to expand our creative problem-solving is to bypass convention and gain insights through comparison.

**1.** List as many answers as you can to the question:

*How is an iceberg like a good idea?*

*Examples*

- You may have to go a long way to find one.
- Most of it doesn't show.

What else?

_____

_____

_____

_____

**2.** Now do the same thing with:

*How is your job like driving a car on the motorway?*

*Examples*

- It's a lot easier if everyone follows procedures.
- If you do it in the afternoon, it's hard to stay awake.

What else?

_____

_____

_____

_____

_____

## Author responses – metaphorical thinking

**1.** *How is an iceberg like a good idea?*

- It floats and moves.
- It is slippery.
- It grows bigger and is anchored at the bottom.
- You'll know it when you see it.
- It has a commanding presence.
- It gets a chilly reception.
- It doesn't show the work that's gone into it.
- It is 90 per cent submerged and to appreciate its magnitude, you have to look below the surface.
- It sometimes melts away.
- It can be moved to other places.
- It's difficult to find.
- It's a wonder of nature.
- When conditions are right, many will be created.

**2.** *How is your job like driving a car on the motorway?*

- It's hard to do if you don't keep your eyes open.
- You have to cooperate with other people.
- Some people go faster than others.
- Some people break the rules.
- It can be noisy and dangerous at times.
- It's confusing until you have done it for a while.
- Sometimes passengers take a nap while you do the work.
- You are in control of the journey. You can pull over, slow down or accelerate.
- It's challenging and exciting sometimes and very routine at others.
- Road signs can help you to stay on the right road.

## Analogy

In science, technology, business, or problem-solving in general, a metaphor frequently provides the key to a new invention or theory. Analogies take metaphoric thinking one step further by creating a comparison between one event or item and something else that has similar elements.

*Example*

- Life *is like* a grapefruit *in that* (or *because*) you just start to enjoy it and it squirts you in the eye.

- Life *is like* reading a good mystery novel *in that* (or *because*) the deeper you get into it, the more you wonder how it will turn out.

When creating analogies and using metaphoric thinking, let your imagination and sense of humour go wild. Have fun! Now it's your turn.

Life is like _____ in that or because _____

_____

53

Life is like _____ in that or because _____

_____

Life is like _____ in that or because _____

_____

Life is like _____ in that or because _____

_____

Life is like _____ in that or because _____

_____

## Problem-solving analogies

A classic example of using an analogy to solve problems is the case of a defence contractor who developed a missile that had to fit so closely within its silo that it couldn't be pushed in. Using the analogy of a horse that refuses to be pushed into a stall, the solution was to lead it in. The solution for the missile company: PULL IT IN WITH A CABLE.

Let's take a look at that process:

**Step 1:** State problem (*What is the situation?*)
Missile fits so closely within silo that it can't be pushed in. How then to get it in?

**Step 2:** Create analogies (*What else* is like *this situation?*)
*Generate as many possibilities as you can, then choose one to work with.*

Trying to get a horse into its stall.
Trying to get toothpaste back into the tube.
Trying to get a fat lady into her girdle.
Trying to get an item back into its shrink-wrap covering.
Trying to get a car into a garage that is too small.

**Step 3:** Solve the analogy
To get a horse that can't be pushed into its stall you need to lead it in.

**Step 4:** Transfer solution to problem
Lead the missile into the silo by pulling it in with a cable.

**Here's a hypothetical problem for you to practise problem-solving with analogy:**

Assume that you are the manager of a large department store. Recently you have been plagued by increasing losses from shoplifting. How can you reduce shoplifting in your store?

**Step 1:** State problem *(What is the situation?)*

**Step 2:** Create analogies

1.
2.
3.
4.
5.

Choose your favourite to work with.

**Step 3:** Solve the analogy

**Step 4:** Transfer solution to problem

A possible solution to this problem is outlined on page 54.

## Author's possible solution using analogies

**Step 1:** *State problem*
How do you keep people from shoplifting?

**Step 2:** *Create analogies*
Trying to keep people from shoplifting *is like*:

1. Trying to keep a cat from eating out of an open can of tuna.
2. Trying to keep children from stealing biscuits from the biscuit tin.
3. Trying to prevent students from cheating in tests.
4. Trying to prevent pedestrians from crossing against the lights.
5. Trying to keep bees away from colourful flowers.

**Step 3:** *Solve the analogy*
Depending on the analogy chosen, a different list of alternatives will become available:

1. How to keep cats from eating out of an open tuna can:
   - cover the can
   - put cat in another room
   - put a dog in the same room
   - put tuna in the refrigerator

2. How to keep children from stealing biscuits from the biscuit tin:
   - hide the tin
   - lock the tin in a cupboard
   - give them some biscuits

3. How to keep students from cheating:
   - isolate them and monitor them closely
   - penalise them when they're caught
   - give oral exams
   - replace tests with projects

4. How to prevent pedestrians from crossing against the lights:
   - erect barriers along the street
   - increase police presence and inst…tute a system of fines
   - increase educational efforts

5. How to keep bees away from colourful flowers:
   - grow the flowers in a greenhouse
   - move the beehive
   - find the bees another source of nectar

**Step 4:** *Transfer solution to problem*
Here are some of the solutions suggested by different analogies:

How to keep people from shoplifting:
- attach electronic anti-theft tags to merchandise that can only be removed by sales staff
- cover the display merchandise with clear plastic
- have a special viewing room for customers
- keep merchandise in a case
- keep all merchandise except a sample in a back room
- give away merchandise (as a reward for catching a shoplifter?)
- instal prominently placed video cameras
- prosecute all shoplifters
- treat shoplifting as an illness
- run support groups and organise lectures from reformed shoplifters
- develop psychological profile of shoplifters for staff of store
- convert store to mail order operation
- move the store to another area less troubled by shoplifters

Name one personal situation in which you'd like to try using analogies to solve a problem.

**Step 1:** *State problem*

**Step 2:** *Create analogies* (Your situation is like _____ )

    1.
    2.
    3.
    4.
    5.

**Step 3:** *Solve the analogy*

**Step 4:** *Transfer solution to problem*

## Personal analogies

To work with personal analogies, you must project yourself into the situation and identify with a person or thing to the extent that you imagine how it would feel to be this person or object. In this exercise there are no right or wrong answers – just your personal insights.

For example, in the case of the shoplifting problem, you might choose to identify with the shoplifter. If so, you'd begin by asking yourself questions and answering *as if* you were the thief:

1. *As the shoplifter, what are my thoughts as I walk into the store?, What do I see, hear, touch, taste, or smell in the shoplifting situation?*
   (Begin with the words, 'As the shoplifter I am motivated to steal something by . . . ' and then continue writing, using the first person. Let your creative imagination take over.)

2. What are your emotions at the moment of taking something?

3. What different types of noises, lights or voices might deter you?

4. What could happen to cause you to change your mind and not take or return the goods?

## Review

Go back over the pages you have written and look for insights that could lead to possible solutions. By using your imagination creatively in this way, you can also identify with objects – writing as if you were the bridge being built or the project being planned.

List at least five current situations where you could gain insight by using the personal analogy: (There are no right or wrong answers.)

1.


2.


3.


4.


5.

## Visual thinking

Visual aids, in various forms, can be used to boost creativity. Try pinning relevant pictures, notes or cartoons on a wall you see regularly. The resulting 'trigger effect' will help your mind to come up with ideas and formulate solutions.

One interesting form of visual thinking is called 'mind mapping'. It is simple to do. Begin by taking a central theme and writing or drawing it in the centre of a sheet of paper. Circle the main theme and draw lines like spokes whenever new ideas come to mind, writing each idea just above the line you have drawn. If one particular idea suggests another association, draw a branch off that line and write it in.

For instance, if you were the owner of a health spa and were looking for ways to develop your business, your mind map might look like this:

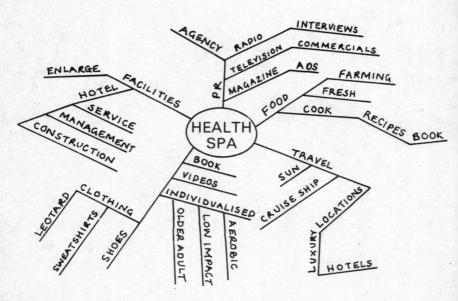

Once you have the knack of letting your mind flow into this visual map, you can use the technique for either business or personal goals. Several corporate executives use mind mapping to prepare informal talks when they have not had time for preparation. One manager used a mind map to decide on the structure and purpose of a project team. As an author, I use mind maps to chart my annual business goals – and put up the maps where I'll see them every day.

## Create your own mind map

Use the space below to experiment with your own mind map. Think about a complex problem in your life and draw a mind map in the space provided below. (Be inventive. Use small drawings or illustrations. Make your spokes different colours.)

# CHAPTER 4
## Group Creativity

## Managing for creativity

Are individuals more creative when working separately or as part of a group? What has your experience been? Of course, it will often depend on the personalities involved, but we often hear of the superior creative efforts of a dedicated group. The product development team of the innovative Macintosh computer at Apple Computer Corporation was one such example. Why then do so many team efforts fall short of the mark? And what can you, as a manager or supervisor, do to increase the creative output of your work teams?

## Build a climate for creativity

A manager must be sensitive to the creative needs of employees and design ways of meeting those needs while still achieving the goals of the organisation. When the following elements are combined, both individual and corporate success is possible. Check your proficiency below.

| I am proficient at: | Do well | Needs improving |
|---|---|---|
| 1. Getting to know employees as individuals and learning their creativity needs. | _____ | _____ |
| 2. Providing training in the basics of creativity for everyone. | _____ | _____ |

| I am proficient at: | Do well | Needs improving |
|---|---|---|
| 3. Guiding and encouraging personal creativity and growth for all. | _____ | _____ |
| 4. Recognising and rewarding creative contributions. | _____ | _____ |
| 5. Ensuring that employees realise that I want and expect creative ideas from everyone. | _____ | _____ |
| 6. Tolerating failure as an expected part of creativity. Making it safe to take risks. | _____ | _____ |
| 7. Reducing the stress level through understanding, empathy, and humour. | _____ | _____ |
| 8. Communicating the mission or vision of the organisation and showing how each function supports it. | _____ | _____ |
| 9. Presenting problem situations as challenging opportunities. | _____ | _____ |
| 10. Inviting creative participation from all those who will be affected by the decision. | _____ | _____ |

Managers who want innovation and creative involvement know how to build a creative climate. If you need to improve – DO IT NOW!

This exercise was adapted from *Team Building* by Robert B Maddux (Kogan Page).

# Idea killers

In order to develop creativity in any group, try to eliminate the following responses to a new idea:

- We have tried it before.
- It would take too long.
- It would cost too much.
- That's not my job.
- That's not your job.
- That's not how we do it here.
- Why don't you put that in writing.
- It's impossible.
- Maybe next year.
- You may be right, but . . .
- That's a stupid idea.
- Our customers would never go for that.
- You can't do that here.
- My mind is definitely made up.
- I don't think that's important.
- Those people don't count.
- I don't need any more information.
- It's good enough.
- 'If it's not broken, don't mend it.'
- Our company is too small.
- Our company is too big.
- We don't have time right now.
- That sounds ridiculous to me.

Add your own.

- 
- 
- 
- 
-

## Idea growers

Idea growers are those individuals who elicit contributions by presenting problems as open-ended opportunities for input. They will often say:

- Are there any questions?
- Before we make a final decision, let's review all the options.
- Where else can we go for additional information on that?
- In the light of the new information, I've changed my mind.
- May I ask a question?
- Excuse me, I don't think I really understood that.
- Is this what you meant?
- I'd like your help with an idea I'm working on.
- How could we improve . . . ?
- What have we missed?
- Who else would be affected?
- What would happen if . . . ?
- Who else has a suggestion?
- Why do we always do it like that?
- Wouldn't it be fun if . . . ?
- I don't know much about that. How about you?
- Let me ask you for some ideas on . . . ?
- How many ways could we . . . ?
- What ideas have you come up with?
- Thank you!

Add your own.

- 
- 
- 
- 
- 
-

# The PPR technique

As a manager who wants to increase the creativity of your staff, the most important question to ask yourself is: 'How do I treat new ideas?' Your management skills may be top notch. In fact, you may even convince everyone that you really want and expect creative contributions. But unless your actions back up your words, you will get nowhere.

It is easy to respond positively to a suggestion or innovation with which you agree. But how do you handle the same enthusiastic contributor who comes up with an idea with which you disagree? Have you ever dismissed an idea so harshly that the person (and anyone else within earshot) is totally demoralised? There is no quicker way to halt creativity from the entire group! On the other hand, you can't accept or endorse every creative suggestion just to protect people's feelings.

The following is a technique that might help. It is called the PPR. The PPR will provide beneficial feedback in situations where you may have reservations about the proposed idea. The first *P* stands for *POSITIVE*. The first thing you do is comment favourably on what you like about the idea. The second *P* is for POSSIBILITIES. This is where you itemise possible applications or extensions of the idea. The *R* represents your *RESERVATIONS* regarding the proposal. You express these in a way that states in a straightforward manner, 'These are my reservations about the project. Can you help me understand how they could be overcome?' By directing the situation back to the person who initiated the idea, you allow them to respond to your concerns by designing a pilot project, building a model, bringing in other examples of similar situations which have been successful etc. You also allow them to reconsider and withdraw the idea.

It's best not to judge others' innovations too critically. An irate banker once told Thomas Edison to 'get that toy out of my office!' so Edison took his invention (the phonograph) somewhere else.

*Case Study 2*
## Handling suggestions

Karen is manager of the women's wear section in a major department store. She has been wanting to improve the customer service and has asked for creative suggestions from her sales group. One of them, Judith, proposed the following: 'I think we should clear a space to put in comfortable chairs and a coffee table with newspapers and magazines. Then the husbands and boyfriends of our customers could wait while their partners try on clothes. It would be even nicer to serve coffee and maybe wine too.'

Karen has some reservations about the suggestion. If she wanted to use the PPR as her evaluation, what might her comments be?

**Positives** (ie 'I like your concern regarding spouses.')
1.
2.
3.
4.
5.

**Possibilities** (ie 'We could have merchandise catalogues for them to read while they wait.')
1.
2.
3.
4.
5.

**Reservations** (ie 'I don't know if we can dismantle our display area to get the extra room needed. How to you think it could be managed?')
1.
2.
3.
4.
5.

(Remember to state these as '*I* have this concern. How could *you* alleviate this for me?')

**Notes to yourself**

In which situations at work do you want to remember to use the PPR technique?

1.
2.
3.
4.
5.

Pick one of these cases and apply the PPR technique.

*Positives*                *Possibilities*                *Reservations*

# Brainstorming

The most popular group creativity technique is Brainstorming. Although it is widely practised, only seldom is it used correctly for optimum benefit. Even if you currently use brainstorming, review these rules to check your technique.

**Preparation:** Prior to the meeting, give each participant a breakdown of the subject to be brainstormed: the problem statement, background information, etc.

Send each participant a set of brainstorming rules.

**Rules:** The ideal group size is between five and twelve people. Ideally, all will be familiar with the procedure. A group leader or facilitator will be in charge of the proceedings, a recorder will write down the ideas expressed (usually on a blackboard or flip chart for the participants to see and review). A time-keeper will also help keep the group moving. The entire group should participate in the idea-generating process.

*Part 1*
Before working on the 'real' situation, it is a good idea to begin with a warm-up exercise (preferably something imaginative or silly to relax and help the group loosen up). When you are ready to set to work, the facilitator should state the problem or situation and invite people to set the ball rolling.

He or she should:

1.  Keep the atmosphere relaxed, fun and free-wheeling.

2. Encourage everyone to participate either with original ideas, or 'piggybacking' (adding on to) other people's suggestions.

3. Concentrate to begin with on quantity, not quality, of ideas. Some groups set a numerical goal (ie 25 or 50 ideas) and try to reach it in the allotted time.

4. Urge participants to say anything that occurs to them, no matter how wild or 'far out' their ideas may seem.

5. Allow sufficient time (20 to 30 minutes) for the idea-generation phase. If the group has been too conservative during this part of the session, the facilitator may use an additional five minutes and ask, 'What are the wildest, most outrageous ideas we can come up with?' (Remember, you may find a gem of an idea that could be adapted to fit reality!)

6. During the idea generation phase, no one should be allowed to judge, criticize or squash any of the ideas generated. The facilitator should be on the lookout for non-productive comments such as, 'We tried that last year,' 'That would cost too much,' 'I don't think that would work,' etc and counter them with, 'This isn't the time for evaluation yet.'

---

**Break:** Before you begin part two of brainstorming, the group should be thanked for their participation in the idea generation phase. Then part one should be brought to a close so the group can take a break before going on. (Indeed, one creative twist that can be effective is to use two groups for generating ideas and swap over lists of possibilities for evaluation by the other group.)

---

*Part 2*

The group should reassemble to assess the input. When this happens, make sure that each member is familiar with the criteria essential for evaluation. For instance, if price, human resources, or timing are important, let everyone know. Look at all ideas and suggestions for the value they might have both as originally stated and if altered slightly. See if you can scale down an outrageous idea to produce one which has practical dimensions.

**Follow up:** Regardless of the results of the session, all team members should be thanked for participating. (A short note may be appropriate.) If ideas were suggested that management decides not to implement, your feedback to the group should be in the form of a PPR response. If a solution that came from the session is accepted, the entire group must receive full credit!

## Brainwriting

With some groups, especially where there is a reluctance to contribute ideas verbally, another technique using written methods, known in the USA as Brainwriting, can replace the more traditional brainstorming. With brainwriting, you follow a similar set of rules, but instead of speaking the ideas out loud, participants will write them down.

**Preparation:** Prior to the meeting, give each participant a breakdown of the subject to be written about: the problem statement, background information etc.

Send each participant a set of 'brainwriting rules'.

**Rules:**   This can be used with a group of almost any size, broken down into sub-groups of four to six. Each group should be seated around a small table. Provide each member of the group with a sheet of paper divided into four columns. A facilitator then explains the rules and announces the amount of time allotted to the session (usually 20 to 30 minutes).

*Part 1*
1. At the top of each piece of paper there should be a brief description of the problem or situation.

2. Participants are instructed to write down four ideas or comments – one in each column.

3. Once a person has completed the four items, he or she puts the paper face down in the centre of the table. When everyone has finished, someone should shuffle the papers and each person picks one that was written by another participant.

4. At this point everyone will have a piece of paper with four items filled in by another person in the group. On this paper the participants write four more items, either additional original ideas or ideas 'piggy-backed' on those on the page. This paper is then returned face down to the centre of the table.

5. This process continues until the participants run out of things to write, no matter how wild or 'far out' their ideas may seem.

> **Break:** Before beginning part two of brainwriting, the group(s) should be thanked for their participation in the idea-generation phase.

*Part 2*
Before the group reassembles to assess the results of the session, a recorder should collect and compile lists of the input. Make sure that each member is familiar with the criteria essential for evaluation. Look at all ideas and suggestions for the value they might have both as originally stated and if altered slightly. See if you can scale down an outrageous idea to produce one with practical dimensions.

**Follow up:** Just as with Brainstorming, team members should be acknowledged and thanked, suggestions not accepted should be commented on, and suggestions accepted should be credited to the group.

## Forced connections

Many products have been developed by forcing a connection between two seemingly unrelated things: some examples include the clock–radio, the wrist watch and the car stereo to name a few. When participants of a group idea-generating session begin to run out of ideas, a facilitator can ask them to look round the room, take something from the environment, and force a connection.

*Example*
Imagine you are part of a product development team looking at ways to improve the common bathtub. What are some improvements your group might come up with?

1. Make it bigger.
2. Route the warm water through pipes to heat the towel rail.
3. Add a snack tray for people who like to eat in the bath.

What else?

4.

5.

6.

7.

8.

9.

10.

When your group runs out of things to say, the facilitator should ask participants to look round the room and select three objects. (*Do this now.*)
What are they?

What ideas might you get for improving a bathtub from each of these things? (A clock might suggest a timer for the bath, a notebook could bring to mind some sort of waterproof pad and marker, a chair could suggest an entirely different shape, etc.)

---

**The 'get fired' technique**

A favourite way to end a group problem-solving session is to ask participants to spend the last few minutes contributing ideas that would probably work, but are so outrageous they could get the group fired. (Obviously, the task then becomes one of scaling or toning down the solution so that the problem is solved without risk to any jobs!)

---

# CHAPTER 5
# Innovation and Practical Solutions

## The politics of creativity

You may have the best creative idea in the history of your organisation. However, unless you know how to persuade others to support and finance your idea it may never see the light. The 'politics' of creativity require a strategic plan which gathers information, convinces key people, builds alliances and obtains reliable feedback.

## Selling your creative ideas

To turn your creative idea into an innovative reality, you must be able to gather the support of key people in your organisation. The following test measures how well you are prepared to sell your idea to the decision-makers.

For each statement below, put a tick under True or False.

|  | True | False |
|---|---|---|
| 1. Being power conscious in your organisation is unworthy of your creative efforts. | ___ | ___ |
| 2. It is impossible to work out what will persuade someone else to support your ideas. | ___ | ___ |
| 3. The only people you will have to sell your ideas to are your superiors. | ___ | ___ |
| 4. It is generally a good plan to give people a 'run-through' of your idea before asking for their support. | ___ | ___ |

*True    False*

5.  One way to gather support for your project is to ask for comments from those you expect to be most affected.

6.  A good idea is often defeated by irrelevant issues.

7.  Unless people are willing to give you total support, it is best to withdraw your request for their help.

8.  It is wise to get more support, resources, capital etc than you think you'll need.

9.  People who 'invest' in your idea will hope to get something in return.

10. It is better to persuade people, even if you have the power to order them to support your idea

11. It is important to convert all your opponents to support of your idea.

12. It is counter-productive to ask for feedback before your idea has been thoroughly thought out.

13. You should be sure to get sole credit for any innovative ideas you create.

14. When selling an idea, one time is as good as another.

15. People are mostly persuaded to back new ideas by the well thought-out details of a presentation.

16. The appraisal of your new idea will probably have nothing to do with power and company politics.

17. The more you know about the people to whom you are selling your idea, the better you can tailor your presentation.

*True   False*

18. It is important for you to support other
    people's good ideas                          ____  ____

19. Unless your idea brings about a major
    change, you should expect little or no
    resistance.                                  ____  ____

20. If you really believe in your idea, you should
    never alter or 'compromise' it.              ____  ____

## Answers to 'Selling your creative ideas'

1. False  Awareness of the power structure of your organi-
          sation is imperative in getting your creative efforts
          recognised.

2. False  While it may be difficult, the more you research and
          can address the needs/concerns of your 'audience',
          the better your chances of success.

3. False  It may be essential ultimately to sell your ideas to
          key executives, but many people at different levels
          in your organisation have the power to help or
          hinder your efforts.

4. True

5. True

6. True

7. False  Many people may only be willing (or able) to give
          limited or conditional support to your project.
          These supporters can still be useful.

8. True

9. True

10. True

11. False  You will probably never be able to convert everyone
           who opposes your idea.

12. False  It can be an opportunity to iron out flaws early if you
           get advance feedback from those whose opinions
           you value.

13. False  A manager once said: 'It is amazing what can be
           accomplished as long as I don't insist on sole credit
           for the innovation.'

14. False  Timing the presentation and the selling of your idea is a crucial part of your strategic plan for success.
15. False  While a solid, logical presentation is important, more people are impressed by the depth of your conviction and enthusiasm.
16. False  It is just as realistic to state that the appraisal of your new idea will have *everything* to do with power and company politics.
17. True
18. True
19. False  Resistance to new ideas should always be anticipated if there is any change.
20. False  Most good ideas have been altered to fit a particular climate or application.

**Interpretation**
Give yourself two points for every correct answer and zero for an incorrect one. Your score represents your overall understanding of what it takes to sell your idea.

| Low level | | Medium level | High level | |
|---|---|---|---|---|
| 0 | 10 | 20 | 30 | 40 |

## Strengthening your presentation

When presenting your new idea, you may bolster your position by citing an outside source. See if you can strengthen your argument by including:

- Examples from other organisations (within or outside your field) which have used a similar idea successfully. If others are doing something similar and it works, your organisation may feel safer in trying it.

- Business and technical journals which have published articles on ideas similar to yours. Quoting from relevant published materials can add credence to your statements.

- Consultants who have experience implementing new ideas in other organisations. Not only can they help you to plan your strategy, they may also be quoted as having unique perspectives on the implementation process of others.

- Company publications in which articles appear on the topic of change, creativity or innovative contributions. If you can use direct statements from top executives that support your position (and then hand out a copy of the article quoted) you may gain strength.

- Recent organisational data including charts, graphs, etc which deal directly with your topic and its cost/added value to the organisation. Looking prepared and informed will boost your creatvity.

## Basic considerations in selling an idea

Success in launching a new idea or programme depends to a large degree on how well you have planned the strategy for 'selling' your idea. The political aspects of your plan require a sensitivity to the power structure in your organisation, especially knowing how your idea addresses the wants or needs of others.

Here are some basic items to consider when developing your strategic plan. Ask yourself these questions early and often!

*What are my personal assets and strengths?* _____

_____

_____

_____

_____

*What are my personal weaknesses and liabilities?* _____

_____

_____

_____

_____

*Who will be affected if my idea gets implemented?* _____

_____

_____

_____

_____

*Who are (or can become) my major allies?* _____

_____

_____

_____

_____

*Who will be my opponents?* _____

_____

_____

_____

_____

*Why will supporters back me?* (How will their interests or reservations be addressed?) _____

_____

_____

_____

*What are the strengths and weaknesses of my opponents?* _____

_____

_____

_____

*Where can I anticipate resistance and how can I minimise its impact?*

_____

_____

_____

_____

*Who will I need to add to my band of supporters?* _____

_____

_____

_____

_____

*How can I attract these individuals?* _____

_____

_____

_____

*Who can I count on for reliable feedback?* _____

_____

_____

_____

*How will the implementation of my idea serve the mission of the
organisation?* _____

_____

_____

_____

*What is the competition doing in this area?* _____

_____

_____

_____

*How much of my idea am I willing to alter?* _____

_____

_____

_____

_____

*How could I implement or test this idea in a way that would minimise the risk to myself and others?* _____

_____

_____

_____

_____

*Why am I so committed to this idea?* _____

_____

_____

_____

_____

## My personal assessment and action plan

The best intentions in the world lead nowhere unless they are put into action. You already have all the creative potential you will ever need. Now it's up to you to apply that creativity in your daily work. By completing this book you are well on your way to increasing your creativity and innovation on the job. You have learned many creative techniques. Where will you use them?

*Current applications of creativity for business*
(Where in your working life do you already express your creativity?)

_____

_____

_____

_____

_____

*Areas in business where you could use more creativity*
(Where do you feel a need for more creativity and innovation?)

_____

_____

_____

_____

_____

*Creativity resources*
(What specific techniques from the book could you use to increase your creativity where it's needed?)

_____

_____

_____

_____

_____

When specifically are you going to put these creativity techniques into action?

**Situation**                                                    **Date**

1. _____

*Creativity technique*

_____

**Situation**

2. _____

*Creativity technique*

_____

**Situation**                                                    **Date**

3. _____

*Creativity technique*

_____


**Situation**

4. _____

*Creativity technique*

_____


**Situation**

5. _____

*Creativity technique*

_____

# Further Reading from Kogan Page

*Effective Meeting Skills*, Marion E Haynes
*Effective Performance Appraisals*, Robert B Maddux
*Effective Presentation Skills*, Steve Mandel
*The Fifty-Minute Supervisor*, Elwood N Chapman
*How to Communicate Effectively*, Bert Decker
*How to Develop a Positive Attitude*, Elwood N Chapman
*How to Develop Assertiveness*, Sam R Lloyd
*How to Motivate People*, Twyla Dell
*Improving Relations at Work*, Elwood N Chapman
*Leadership Skills for Women*, Marilyn Manning and
    Patricia Haddock
*Make Every Minute Count*, Marion E Haynes
*Managing Disagreement Constructively*, Herbert S Kindler
*Sales Training Basics*, Elwood N Chapman
*Speak With Confidence*, Meribeth Bunch
*Successful Negotiation*, Robert B Maddux
*Team Building*, Robert B Maddux
*Ten Keys to Dynamic Customer Relations*, Gregory H Sorensen

Please write to the publishers for a full list of their business
and management titles.